A LIGHTER SHADE OF BLUE

Other Books by Scott Baker and Tom Philbin

The Funniest Cop Stories Ever

A LIGHTER SHADE OF BLUE

Scott Baker and Tom Philbin

**Andrews McMeel
Publishing, LLC**

Kansas City • Sydney • London

Andrews McMeel Publishing, LLC
an Andrews McMeel Universal company
1130 Walnut Street, Kansas City, Missouri 64106

www.andrewsmcmeel.com

11 12 13 14 MLT 10 9 8 7 6 5 4 3 2 1

ISBN: 978-1-4494-0774-2

Library of Congress Control Number: 2011926176

ATTENTION: SCHOOLS AND BUSINESSES
Andrews McMeel books are available at quantity discounts with bulk purchase for educational, business, or sales promotional use. For information, please e-mail the Andrews McMeel Publishing Special Sales Department:
specialsales@amuniversal.com

To my father.
The older I become, the more my respect for your wisdom, character, and charm becomes immeasurable.

To my mother.
You kept on cheering long after the laughter had stopped.
I thank you and love you both.

To all the men and women who wear the uniform
and who shared these stories with us.
Don't take the job home with you,
laugh when you can, and stay safe.

—Scott Baker

INTRODUCTION

It takes a variety of attributes to become a good cop—things like courage, integrity, honor, and compassion. One of the most often overlooked attributes, though, is a sense of humor. How important is it?

I believe that if a cop doesn't have one, he might as well turn in his service weapon because without it he'll go crazy within six months.

A sense of humor comes into play at the oddest times, such as during a high-speed chase, a family dispute, the foot pursuit of an ostrich, or even at a murder scene. When things are so tense that cops are ready to explode, laughter can and does diffuse the situation.

I really loved being a New York City cop. I was in the belly of the beast in the greatest city in the world. It gave me a chance to fulfill my thrill-seeking side, to help people in need, to feel like I was contributing to society by making it a better place, and to witness firsthand some of the funniest situations you could ever imagine. A few years ago I gathered some stories and published them in a book called *The Funniest Cop Stories Ever*. Lots of cops from all over the world read it and sent me *their* stories, which we've included in this book. The tales are varied. Some are warped, some are wacky, and some are weird, but all are funny!

The stories are in cops' own words. Only the names have been changed to protect the insane—and by that I do mean the cops. Enjoy!

A LIGHTER SHADE OF BLUE

NOT FOR EVERYBODY

The NYPD is not for everybody. We get this one kid named Anderson from East Cupcake—that's what we call kids who come on the job from the soft suburbs and have never seen the hard streets of the inner city. He's fresh out of the academy, and he gets assigned to my command in a tough area we call "Do or Die Bed-Stuy" [Bedford-Stuyvesant, Brooklyn].

I was the patrol supervisor one day and I had to give all the cops a scratch—cop talk for signing their memo books to show I checked up on them. I get to Anderson, and I ask him if everything is OK. He says, "Not really. I think I am going to quit."

I say, "Quit? You just went through six months in the academy and you're going to quit? Why?"

"Well, it's my first day out here, and I responded to two shootings and a knife fight. I mean, is that normal?"

I say, "No, it's not normal. Give it a few weeks and see how you feel."

The next day I am on the desk, and Anderson comes storming in, slams his badge down, and starts to unload his gun and hand it to me. He is screaming.

"I f——n' quit and you're an f——n' liar!"

I ask, "What are you talking about?"

"Yesterday I responded to two shootings and a knife fight, and you said that wasn't normal. Today it was three shootings, an assault with a bottle, a DOA [dead body] in the trunk of a car, and a fight between two guys with baseball bats!"

I stand up and yell back, "I didn't f——n' lie to you. Yesterday *wasn't* normal—that's a slow day. *Today* was normal!"

BUT NOT DEAF

We were on patrol on a late tour driving down 204th Street toward Webster Avenue in the Bronx. All of a sudden I get flagged down by a girl in her midtwenties who says she is an off-duty nurse and saw a man fall on the corner in front of Gorman's Bar. We go and take a look and there is this old guy lying there with a gash on his head. We call for a bus [ambulance], and while we're waiting, the nurse props the guy up so that his back is resting against her shins. She then leans over and starts asking questions loudly in his ear to see if he is coherent.

"What's your name?" she asks. There is no response.

Then, a little louder: "Who is the president of the United States?"

No response.

She starts actually *yelling* more questions, and he finally looks up at me and says in a loud, slurred thick brogue, "Officer, will you tell this bitch that I'm drunk, not deaf!"

SIMPLE SOLUTION

I was working a U2 concert detail in Ireland when Bono asks the audience for quiet. Then, in the silence, he starts to slowly clap his hands and says, "Every time I clap my hands, a child in Africa dies."

A voice from near the front of the audience yells, "Well, stop your fookin' clapping then!"

THE RAZOR'S EDGE

Me and my partner, Raymo, were working undercover narcotics one time, and we got called down to court to go to a grand jury. Since we were undercover, we had the long hair and beards, but the ADA [assistant district attorney] handling the case wanted us to come in clean-shaven. No problem. We figure we would stop in a barbershop on our way to court and get it taken care of.

We hit this barbershop and the receptionist is this really good-looking woman. Cops can be notorious flirters. Raymo is a good-looking single guy, so he is flirting with her while he is getting his hair cut. Now my shave is done and Raymo's haircut is done so the two barbers switch. Raymo's new barber comes over to lather him up for his shave, and Raymo asks the receptionist, "Hey, I have to head over to court after this but whaddaya say when I'm done I come back and grab ya for a drink?"

She says, "I don't think so."

Now the barber kicks Raymo's chair back and tells him not to talk as he lathers him up and sharpens his razor. But Raymo keeps talking and asks, "Why not?"

She responds, "Because I'm married."

"So it's just a cup of coffee. We don't have to tell your husband."

She answers back, "You just did. He's the guy about to shave you."

THE COLANDER ALWAYS TELLS THE TRUTH!

Police in Radnor, Pennsylvania, interrogated a suspect by placing a metal colander on his head and connecting it to a photocopy machine with telephone wires. The message "He's lying" was placed in the copier, and the cops pressed the copy button each time they thought the suspect wasn't telling the truth. Believing the "lie detector" was working, the suspect confessed.

THE ULTIMATE SIN

We respond to an assault in progress. One drunk is stabbed and on the floor with the knife still sticking in his upper left arm. The perp is drunk also. There's a broad that looks like she weighs about sixty pounds, *maybe* sixty-five pounds. She has more track marks than Grand Central Station.

Turns out that the guy who got stabbed had slept with the other guy's "wimmin" in the past.

"So you caught him screwin' your old lady again?"

"No, Officer, this time I caught him drinking my wine."

"Are you kiddin' me? He screws your old lady and you give him a warning and admonish. Now you catch him drinking your wine and you damn near take his arm off?"

"Officer, I don't care if he bones my old lady. I mean, she ain't exactly no prize. *But this is damn good wine!*"

COLLARED

Back in the '70s, we were called to a domestic dispute at a familiar address. This woman would always call us to play referee but never wanted her husband locked up. He would get drunk, get caught with another woman, and a physical fight would break out but never with any serious injuries. This was back in the day before the laws changed to a "*must*-arrest situation." This time when we got there, the wife had some scratches on her face, but she said the scratches were not from her husband.

"Then who are they from?" I asked.

"My cat scratched me."

My partner, Smitty, and I were fed up with this family and all the BS every week, so I say, "That sounds a little outlandish."

"You calling me a liar?" she says.

"You're sure the cat did it?"

"Absolutely."

At this point the woman had pissed me off. She's lying to me and she's wasting my time. So I said, "We're going to have put the cat under arrest."

"What? You crazy!"

"Watch me."

With that I take the cuffs off my belt, and my partner picks up and holds the cat. I fasten the cuffs on his collar, and as I do, I announce that he's under arrest for *feline-ius* assault with his claws. Then I make up some law and tell her the city will be charging her one hundred dollars a day as a boarding fee until the cat can be deemed safe. The city is backed up, so it could take up to thirty days for an animal psychologist to make that determination. She starts freaking out.

"That's three thousand dollars, you jackasses! Hell, it only cost a hundred bucks to bail my husband out of jail!" Then she starts shouting, "OK, OK, my husband did it, and his drunk ass is passed out in the bedroom. Now let my cat go!"

MAYBE YOU'RE BETTER OFF

M y partner, Tommy, and I get a call about a male barricaded in an apartment. The procedure is to check it out to see if it is a dangerous situation or an EDP [emotionally disturbed person], in which case we are supposed to call a patrol supervisor and wait for an ESU [emergency service unit].

We show up and a neighbor meets us and tells us the situation. He says, "The guy is really depressed over his girlfriend leaving, and he's threatening to kill himself."

"OK, what's his name?" I ask.

"Frank."

I thank him, and Tommy and I figure while we wait for the ESU maybe we can calm things down. We knock on his door, and the guy yells, "Leave me the bleep alone, or I'll blow my brains out!"

I say, "Whoa, slow down, Frank. What's the problem? Maybe we can work it out."

"No, nobody can help me. It's my girlfriend. She left me, and she is everything to me."

I say, "Come on, Frank. She is not worth killing yourself. There are all kinds of other women out there waiting for you to tickle their tuna."

"You don't understand! She was the best! When my father died she was there for me, when I lost my job she helped me, when I was sick she took care of me, when my dog died she comforted me."

Tommy, who was quiet through all this, finally says in his Brooklynese accent, "Hey, Frankie, not for nuttin', but this broad sounds like bad luck. Maybe you're better off without her?"

It broke the ice, and he came out when the ESU showed up.

A NEW YORK MOMENT

Only in New York could this happen. We were working in Midtown North in the theater district, and one night we get a call of an assault, which could mean a lot of different things. We pull up by Eighth Avenue and, as we do, this beefy-sized woman waves us down. As we pull closer, the "woman" is coming more and more into focus. We can see that her dress is torn a bit, her knees are scraped, her stockings ripped, and she's generally disheveled.

She starts to tell me what happened in this deep voice, and it seems obvious she's a transvestite. But she's a straight guy, a Broadway actor. He tells us he just did a promo shoot for his play and everybody left, and he walked alone a few blocks back to the theater. Then some jerk tried to grab his pocketbook and run.

He says, "I know there was nothing in the pocketbook but instinct made me fight to hold on to it. So I am fighting with this guy, but he got away because my dress was too tight and I can't fight in these shoes."

Now we are all laughing about this "only in New York" type moment.

I ask him for a description and he tells me, "Hmmm, white guy, age twenty-five to thirty, brown eyes, brown hair, and about my height."

Well, the guy was pretty tall so I ask, "About six feet?"

He says, "No, five-eight." Then he kicks off his shoes and drops four inches and says, "I was wearing my heels when he mugged me."

SMART ANSWER

As cops, we are always rotating tours and days off. It gets really confusing sometimes, to the point that you don't even know what day it is. Well, me and my partner are doing a day tour, and it was about 1100 hours [11 a.m.] when a description comes over the radio of two youths who just did a robbery about three blocks away. We turn the corner, spot two kids who fit the description, and we pull up to where they are and start to question them. They are giving us a lot of attitude and starting to piss me off, and I am thinking these kids are definitely dirty. Innocent people usually cooperate and then go on their way. So we keep them there and the other unit brings the victim to us to ID the kids we stopped. He takes one look and says, "No, that ain't them, no way."

So now this totally fires up the kids, and they start going ape: "Why you stoppin' us?! Yo, this is harassment! We didn't do nothin'! I'm suing the police!"

So I yell back, "Shut up! If you clowns were in school today, you wouldn't even have been stopped!"

The kid looks at me and says, "Yo, Five-oh, it's Saturday. There ain't no school today."

Now I feel like an idiot, but I make a quick recovery and yell back, "Yeah, well, you're so stupid you should go to school on the weekends, too!"

IT'S FOUR O'CLOCK— DO YOU KNOW WHERE YOUR CHIMP IS?

In 1980, I lived on the beat that I patrolled. It had a combination of businesses, apartments, and beautiful tree-lined residential streets. One afternoon, my partner and I answer a call to a home where a woman has reported a chimpanzee running in and out of her house. Of course, the dispatcher's voice registered her personal disbelief, and we got a lot of "clicks" on the radio from other officers expressing the same opinion. Everyone thought the complainant might be a crackpot.

When we got there, this terrified woman comes running up to us, and simultaneously we see a chimpanzee running in and out of the woman's house. I didn't know how to deal with it. Chimp 101 is not the kind of thing they teach in the academy. My partner looks at me and asks, "What the hell are we gonna do?" I ask the woman for a banana and give it to my partner to try and coax the chimp down from the roof. He asks me if I think it will work, and I say, "I dunno. I saw it work on the Magilla Gorilla cartoon as a kid—we might as well try it." Then I remember a pet store a couple of blocks away that advertises chimp shows for kids' parties, so I call and get the owner on the line.

I said, "It's four o'clock. Do you know where your chimp is?"

Then I get serious and tell him the story. The worried owner realizes instantly that it is his chimp and says he'll be right over. When I get back, I see my partner is going toe to toe with the chimp, who's trying to get the banana from him while my partner is trying to grab his collar. Later, we found out that one of the tricks the owner taught the chimp was a Western scene where there is fake shootout, and the chimp plays dead. So thinking my partner's gun was a toy, the chimp went for it! They are going around and around in a circle with the chimp trying to grab the gun, and my partner trying to give him the banana!

Fortunately, the owner arrived quickly and told the chimp to let go of the gun and leashed him up.

My partner was pissed at me for giving him the banana to bait the chimp. I said, "What are you so pissed about? I was inside doing all the thinking and legwork to find the owner, and you are out here monkeying around!"

DIST ID	D.C. NO.	SECT.	DIST.	REPORT DATE
KCM006-A	20	HMR	980-09-12	10/20/2011

Adding Insult to Injury

One Suffolk County, Long Island, cop said, "A few years ago in Huntington we ran across a guy who should be in one of those dumbest criminal books, but it would be posthumously. He burglarized an office and tried to wrestle a six-hundred-pound safe down a flight of stairs. He lost control, and the safe crushed him. To add insult to injury, there was nothing valuable in the safe—just insurance forms."

REPORT PREPARED BY *John Law* NO. 483000120

ROAM AWAY

My partner, Pete, is a quick-witted guy, but he has a sense of humor that some people don't get, and this can get us in trouble. Like one night we were on patrol and stopped to write a summons to a double-parked car blocking traffic. That's when we were approached by a goth-looking woman in her twenties who was walking her dog. She stops in front of us and says, "Hey, I know who owns this car. Don't write him a ticket. Don't you guys have anything better to do?"

We just ignore the comment, which gets her even more worked up, so then she asks sarcastically, "Is there a leash law on the books in New York or are you gonna write me a ticket for that, too?"

"No," Pete says with a straight face, "there isn't. You can roam the streets as long as you want."

PREY

Another cop told me a story that he swears is true.

A young woman came home and placed her engagement ring, worth over a grand, on the edge of the kitchen sink and started to wash her hands. She accidentally bumped the ring, and it disappeared down the drain.

Panicked, she went into the bedroom and woke up her husband and told him what had happened. The husband, a handy guy, said the ring might be in the trap, a curved piece on the bottom of the piping.

"I better check," he said. "Otherwise, we may forget, run the water, and the ring will wash down and will be gone."

Then—nude—he gets out of bed, gets his tools, goes over to the sink, and lies on his back, his head looking straight up at the trap. Then he starts to disassemble it.

Unknown to him, the family cat has silently walked up to view the scene and started to get preoccupied with the husband's genitalia, which moved a little every time the husband moved. The cat must have thought it was prey. Interest turned to action,

and the cat leaped on the husband's genitals, which made
the husband's head spasm up at warp speed and hit the trap,
knocking him unconscious. The wife called 911, and EMTs came
and revived him.

CAPTAIN NAKED

One night back in the '60s, my partner, Ritchie, and I collared a real wise guy for mugging some middle-aged woman, and we brought him into the station to book him. This guy seemed to have a personal thing against my partner, and he kept calling him a motherf——r, even after we locked him up in the cage. Ritchie is very low-key, but I could see that as the guy kept cursing at him, he was getting worked up. Finally he tells the guy, "If you say that to me one more time, you will deeply regret it."

So what does the perp go and do? He calls him a motherf——r, twice.

Ritchie blinks once and calmly states, "I'll be right back," and walks out of the room. Now I am there with the perp for about five minutes, wondering where the hell my partner is. All of a sudden Ritchie bursts through the door wearing nothing but black dress socks, his shoes, and a police cap and carrying a billy club.

The guy yells, "*Holy crap!* What the hell you doin'? Why are you naked?"

Ritchie says, "So I won't get your blood spattered on my uniform!"

I jump in and play good cop, pretending to try to stop Ritchie from killing this kid. I am holding Ritchie back and yelling to the perp, "Oh, man, you did it. Now my partner is going to beat you like a dirty rug! You better apologize!"

Scared to death, the kid starts yelling, "OK, OK, I'm sorry. I won't use that language again. Now please put on some clothes!"

From then on Ritchie had a new nickname: Captain Naked.

YELLOW WITH PINK POLKA DOTS

This one old-time cop Eddie who lived in my sector told me that back in the '30s and '40s when he was on the job, some detectives would revert to backroom confessions. You know, slap a guy around a bit to see if he would crack. I'm not saying it was right or fair, but it did happen from time to time. So he told me this story of one detective he worked with named Paul who had a rubber hose he would use, but he painted it all types of unusual colors. Eddie asked Paul why he did that, but all he said was "You'll see why one day."

So they get this perp on a burglary collar and bring him in, but he won't give them any information. Paul leaves the room for a minute and comes back with the multicolored rubber hose and uses it on the perp, who promptly confesses to everything. So they end up in court with the guy telling the judge the confession was beaten out of him, even though he didn't have any marks on him.

"What did they do?" the judge asked.

"At one point they put a Manhattan telephone book on my belly and then beat it with a piece of rubber hose."

Now the judge is concerned; accusations like that are taken seriously. "Can you describe the hose?" he asks.

"Sure, it was about two feet long, and yellow with pink polka dots."

Now the judge looks down over his glasses and asks angrily, "How about the suit the guy using the hose was wearing? Was it the same colors? Or was he dressed like a clown maybe? Get this nut out of my courtroom!"

FRESH START

We were doing a four-by-twelve tour [4 p.m. to midnight] when a robbery comes over the radio. My partner and I were too far away from the scene to get there in time to intervene, so we got the description of the perp and decided to canvas the surrounding areas for him. Right away, we spot a guy who fits the description, so we roll up on him. He is trying to play it real cool, but you could tell he was real nervous. My partner asks for his ID, and the guy starts yelling, "This s——t ain't even right. I ain't no criminal."

So we tell him why we stopped him and ask for his ID again. He gives us an inmate card, which shows that he was paroled the day before after serving time for robbery.

I say, "You're yelling at us that you're not a criminal, but you were just paroled yesterday after doing a bit for robbery."

This guy had big glassy eyes. They slide craftily from one side of his head to the other, and he says, "Yeah, well, um . . . I ain't no criminal no more."

DIST ID	D.C. NO.	SECT.	DIST.	REPORT DATE
KCM006-A	28	HMR	980-09-12	10/28/2011

The Secret's in the Sauce

Serial killers Ottis Toole and Henry Lee Lucas were friends. A Texas cop said that Toole and Lucas would kill and barbecue some victims, which only Toole would eat. A cop asked Lucas why he didn't join Toole in these unholy feasts.

Lucas answered, "I don't like barbecue sauce."

REPORT PREPARED BY *(signature)*   NO. 483000128

A NEW KIND OF STIMULUS

We were doing a midnight tour on a Tuesday one time when me and my partner, Danny, had to answer a call about a ringing alarm, which turned out to be false, in the industrial part of the precinct. This area usually has a lot of "ladies of the evening" out, but at this late hour they are usually off the streets. So I was pretty surprised to see one of the regulars named Beverly. We pull over, and I shout out, "Hey, Bev, what are you doin' out this late, sugar?"

She smirks and walks over to the RMP [radio mobile patrol car] and says, "Man, you know, Five-oh, times are rough. I gotta put in a little ova time, baby."

Danny says to her, "What's the matter? Congress's stimulus package hasn't trickled down to the workin' woman yet?"

She looks at us bewildered and says, "What? Look, I don't know what y'all talkin' 'bout, but I haven't stimulated *anyone's* package all night!"

WANTS TO *REALLY* GO UNDERCOVER

When I was working in OCCB [the Organized Crime Control Bureau], we put a bug in a wiseguy's house in Staten Island, and we would sit in an unmarked van around the corner listening in. Most of these wiseguys have a goomah on the side, you know a girlfriend, and one day we hear a fight break out. The wife is *seething* and she tells him, "Every time I turn around, you are in another woman's pants. How would you like it if I screwed everything that came my way? You remember when we were in Italy, and you were running with your 'business associates' and left me alone in the hotel? A lot of hot Italian men were hitting on me, and I didn't do a damn thing. I should have slept with all of them! Trust me, I am gonna screw the first guy I see—I don't care if it's a damn stranger!"

The wiseguy had had enough of this verbal assault, and we hear him say good-bye and leave. So Andy, one of the detectives in the van with us, says, "I need to stretch my legs," and he steps outside and just walks, something that is not uncommon when you are sitting undercover for eight to ten hours in a small space. He ultimately disappears around the corner.

About ten minutes go by, and we hear the bell ring on the bug. The lady goes to the door, and sure enough, we hear Andy's voice but with an Italian accent: "*Buon giorno!* Scuse me, I'm a-lost. Can you a-give me *direcciones*?"

We were cracking up.

WHERE IT'S SAFER

We were in an RMP on the Grand Concourse in the Bronx when we see a car weaving so wild it went into the oncoming lane. So we hit the bubble lights and siren and pull the car over. It's a middle-aged guy, and you didn't need a Breathalyzer to realize that he is totally hammered.

"Hey," I said, "you've been drinking?"

"Yeah," he said, the word badly slurred.

"Why are you driving?"

"Well, I tried to walk home but it was too dangerous. I kept falling down!"

DIST ID	D.C. NO.	SECT.	DIST.	REPORT DATE
KCM006-A	33	HMR	980-09-12	12/10/2009

Logical, No?

A Texas cop questioning Henry Lee Lucas asked him, "How come you have sex with women only after you kill them?"

Lucas answered, "I like peace and quiet."

REPORT PREPARED BY

NO. 97253633

ME AND MY TWO FRIENDS

When you go on a post for the first time, some of the punks will test you, see if they can intimidate you, and that happened to me. A trio of these jerks came up to me and start telling me how they could make my life miserable—that they outnumbered me.

"No, you don't," I said. "I have two friends with me."

The bozo talking looked puzzled. "Where are they?"

"On my hip," I said, patting my weapon. "Smith and Wesson."

THE PUNCHING PREACHER

When I was working in the East Village back in the early '80s the precinct's nickname was "the Evil." It was full of junkies, yuppies, prostitutes, millionaires, gangsters, and people who should have been institutionalized, and they all seemed to have a reason to come into our station house at one time or another. The desk sergeant, with twenty-three years on the job, was named Pellegrino, and he took it all in stride. Nothing seemed to get to him, and he had a great dry sense of humor.

I remember an incident involving him and a guy we called "the Punching Preacher." He had long hair, a beard, beads, the whole bit, and he was six-foot-six and weighed around 250 pounds. He used to be a boxer but now was a self-ordained minister.

One hot night the Punching Preacher comes bursting into the room and goes up to each person there yelling, "Have you found Jesus? Have you found Jesus?!" Then he goes to the desk where Pellegrino is and yells, "Sergeant, have you found Jesus?"

Pellegrino shakes his head and says, "No, but I'll notify Missing Persons and have them get on it."

"Bless you, Sergeant."

THE PUNCHING PREACHER RETURNS

One time in the dead of winter, the Punching Preacher comes running into the station house dressed in long johns with his boxing trunks pulled over them, frantically waving his arms and yelling, "Jesus is coming! Jesus is coming! *He* is on his way. Jesus is coming!!"

Sergeant Pellegrino has his head down and is making entries in the logbook. He pauses, looks over the tops of his glasses, and says, "Great. We have two sector cars knocked out, so tell him to stop wasting time, grab a radio, and start picking up jobs!"

"Bless you, Sergeant."

HUH?

So I lock up this woman for some petty BS one time, and
while I'm filling out the OLBS [online booking sheet]
I'm asking this female perp the questions on the form.
After each question I get the usual highly educated
response of "Huh?" I swear to God she said it so many
times--Huh? Huh? Huh? Huh?--it sounded like I was
processing a bunch of geese.

When I got to the part on the OLBS where it asks,
"Are you a U.S. citizen?" the woman says, "Huh?" again.
I'm so fed up, I ask loudly, "It's very simple! What
state were you born in?"

She looks at me and yells, "United States!"

YOUR ATTENTION, PLEASE!

When you work midnights, your sleeping patterns get all screwed up. Most guys like me and Tommy D. try to get some sleep before we come on duty, but this one night Tommy went fishing for the whole day. When he came in, he said, "Jimmy, only pick up jobs if it's a must. I'm completely shot."

"Yeah, yeah, no problem," I tell him. "You sack out. I'll drive, and we'll hope for a slow night."

Minutes into the tour, Tommy is passed out and starts snoring up a storm so loud he could set off car alarms. At around 4 a.m., after four hours of his snoring, I decided I'd had enough. I see this garbage truck idling with its headlights on. I quietly put the patrol car in park, and I go tell the guy in the truck, "Listen, when you see me put the cop lights on, just do me a favor and hit your horn as hard as you can."

"It's an air horn," the guy says. "It can wake up the dead."

"That's the idea."

The guy agrees. Then I get back in the patrol car and roll right in front of the garbage truck so the truck's headlights are facing the passenger door and lighting up Tommy. I slam the brakes, hit the lights, and the garbage truck driver hits the horn so loud it almost made my ears bleed. I scream, *"Oh my God, Tommy, watch out!"*

His eyes snap open, and he screams at the top of his lungs. He was so startled, he jumped up and hit his head on the window and nearly knocked himself out. I was laughing so hard at the look on his face, I could hardly breathe.

KENNY MUST BE THE SMART ONE!

DEPUTY

I did this when I was on patrol in Crown Heights. My partner, Kenny, was on vacation, so I was partnered up with a great kid who was asking lots of questions and regarded me as a great GLA [grand larceny auto] guy. The kid kept asking me, "How do you and Kenny get so many GLAs?"

This was back in the day before we had computers in all the cars to run plates. It's really just experience and some luck, to be honest, but, I figure, why not make myself look smart and scientific *and* have some fun with the kid all at once? So I tell him, "Well, to be honest, there are certain codes to look for and secret methods not many people know about. It could take *years* to learn, but if you really want to know, I guess I could show you."

The rookie says with wide eyes, "Thanks, that would be great!"

It was raining out; in fact, pouring. I pull up next to a car and I tell the kid, "OK, write down the VIN [vehicle identification number]—it's on the registration sticker." He exits the car and writes it down, then gets back in the RMP pretty much soaked and hands me the number. I look at the number, rub my chin wisely, and say the thirteen numbers out loud and finally proclaim, "Nah, this car is good."

We drive down a few streets, and I pull up to another car and tell him to do the same thing, and he does. I say, "Oh, damn! This one was close. I actually thought it was stolen, but it checks out." This goes on for the better part of the tour, and each time I announce something different with the VIN—make some kind of long division equation on paper, circle certain numbers and letters, make up stuff that is complicated and meaningless gibberish that sounds impressive, like "I'm gonna do the Beckendorff configuration on this car because it's a Mercedes, a German car." Each time concluding, "Nah, this car is good."

I can tell he's getting frustrated, and he's completely drenched, like a rat that just swam the East River. So I say, "You want to try one more?"

The kid turns to me, his eyes on fire. "Listen, man, I'm soaked. I don't think you know shit about stolen cars! Kenny must be the smart one!"

COMBINATION PLATTER

I was with the NYPD, and one of my first assignments back in the early '70s was a foot post at Bowery and Delancey, on the Lower East Side. We were on the twelve-to-eight tour, and due to a precinct condition, our basic job was to keep the ladies of the evening—50 percent of them being guys in drag—moving and from gathering at that particular intersection.

One particular night, we arrested about seven or eight hookers, some of them of the male persuasion. They were transported to the Fifth Precinct, where we had to babysit them until court in the morning. NYPD policy is that, if possible, a female officer must search a female prisoner for weapons and contraband. We placed them all in one room, and let me tell you, some of the "he-shes" looked better than the real thing. I mean, it was real tough to tell the difference on some of them. I located a rookie female officer fresh out of the academy, and I asked her to toss [cop slang for search] the female prisoners. One by one we sent the ladies into the ladies' room, including one bodacious Asian with very large breasts, and we could hear the rookie officer say, "Assume the position." When she patted down the prisoner and reached her crotch, we knew she had felt a bulge.

She says, "What is this, a weapon? Lift up your skirt."

In shock, the rookie female yells out, "What the hell?! You have tits *and* a penis!" The Asian he-she took it all in stride.

"That's right, honey, I'm a combination platter. My customers can order off column A or column B."

WHAT A TOUGH GUY! WOW!

One time we were sitting on a bug in a trailer in a Bronx landfill. It was the headquarters of two Mafia capos, named Joe Zingaro and John "Buster" Ardito. One day, we hear this gofer-type guy yelling and screaming at Joe and Buster.

"Hey, you two f——n' punks are half the man I am, and you treat me with no respect! I should chop your f——n' balls off and cut youse into little pieces and trow da both of your sorry asses into da bay! Don't youse eva show me no disrespect again or I swear I will embarrass da both of yas," and so on and so on. We expect to hear the sound of gunfire at any time.

But it doesn't come, and me and my partner, Nicky C., are just looking at each other, thinking like, "Wow! How does this guy have the balls to say these things to these two heavy hitters? What a tough guy! And how are Zingaro and Ardito taking all this without answering back?" Then all of a sudden, we hear the trailer door opening and the gofer saying, smiley and respectful, "Hey, Joe. Hey, John. How's it going, fellas? Good to see ya!"

DIST ID	D.C. NO.	SECT.	DIST.	REPORT DATE
KCM006-A	45	HMR	980-09-12	9/4/2001

Yikes!

A mother called 911. She was very worried and asked the dispatcher if she needed to take her kid to the emergency room, since the kid was eating ants. The dispatcher says, "Just give the child some Benadryl, and it should be fine."

"I just gave him some ant killer," the mother says.

"What? Rush him to the emergency room!" the dispatcher hollers.

The kid survived, and so did the 911 operator.

REPORT PREPARED BY	NO.
	97253645

NOBODY WANTED MY CANDY

We had this one sergeant who was a good guy but a real prankster, so we had to try and mess with him. One Halloween, a guy took a piece of white paper and a black Sharpie, cut the paper into the size and shape of a license plate, and wrote "I love young boys" on the "plate" and taped it over the sergeant's rear license plate on his personal car.

The sergeant drove around like that for about three days, until a neighbor knocked on his door and asked, "Hey, Jim, are you working undercover or something trying to catch predators?"

"No, why?"

Then the neighbor pointed out the sign on the license plate. The sergeant raises an eyebrow and says, "Well, that explains why I didn't get any trick-or-treaters this year—and why my car was egged."

CALL ME AN AMBULANCE!

After chasing a drunk driver for about twenty minutes
in his RMP in the middle of the night, a cop watches
the guy drive through a store window. The drunk gets
out of the smashed-up car, sees that he's been cut by
the broken glass and is bleeding, and collapses. Then
he sees the officer and screams, "Call me an ambulance!
Call me an ambulance!"

So the cop says, "OK, you're an ambulance."

THANK HEAVEN FOR THE SENTENCE REDUCTION!

I was a guard—one of many—at the 1988 sentencing of Jimmy Coonan, head of the Westies gang and one of the most fearsome American gangsters of all time. He was a cold-blooded murderer. This guy would chop you up and dump you in the river if you even so much as looked at him the wrong way. Federal prosecutor Mary Lee Warren characterized his crimes as "off the scale."

At any rate, they nailed him under the RICO statute, and the judge was Whitman Knapp, a very old man but still tough and very sharp.

Before he was sentenced, Coonan stood in front of Knapp and read a statement about how sorry he was for everything he had done and how he had hurt his family and the families of all the victims he murdered. When he was finished, Knapp thanked him sincerely for the statement, but he was unmoved and proceeded to sentence Coonan to 150 years in prison. We take Coonan out of the courtroom, and he is waiting to go back to jail when Kenny, one of the other guards, says sarcastically, "Hey, Coonan, only a hundred and fifty years? Wow! Good thing you read your statement. He could have given you life—nice job, you smooth talker."

WE DON'T EAT JUST DOUGHNUTS

One night on patrol in Corona, I was riding with this old-timer named Philly C. He was a pretty nice guy, but he had like thirty-plus years on the job and didn't take crap from anyone. He usually drove the sergeant, who was his ex-partner years ago when they both worked in Brooklyn. However, tonight the sergeant was on the desk, and my partner was out, so the sergeant put me and Philly C. together.

Shortly, we see a double-parker. We get out and start to write him up, and the owner of the car comes running up, cursing Philly C. out. That's the wrong thing to do with a cop who can retire on the spot. Philly C. doesn't get angry; he just asks for the guy's license. The guy is still cursing as he digs it out of his wallet and hands it over. Instead of giving him the ticket, Philly C. just smiles and eats the guy's license! The guy is going nuts, and as we walk back to the patrol car Philly C. yells, "Hey, look on the bright side. You talked me out of a ticket." The guy is so pissed, he runs into the police station and tells the desk sergeant what happened. The sergeant asks the guy, "Well, did you get a ticket?"

The guy says, "No."

The sergeant stands up behind the desk and yells at the guy, "Well, then stop f——n' whining and get the hell out of here before I eat your registration, too!"

THE CHOICE IS YOURS, LAD

In the '60s, it was a lot different for cops as far as information-gathering techniques went. From time to time, there were "backroom confessions." That means when cops knew a perp was guilty or had vital information on a crime, rumor had it they might occasionally use force or the threat of force to make a subject give up that information.

An old-time cop described how they were trying to get this one kid to talk. He didn't commit the crime, but he knew his friends did. So they question him mildly for a while, but he still won't sing, keeping up his tough-guy attitude to protect his image and his friends. The arresting officer then brings him upstairs and puts him in an interrogation room. They let him sit there awhile; then two big old-time Irish detectives walk in. They don't say a word for about a minute as they circle the table, slowly putting on some leather gloves and slamming a rubber hose on the table. They each light a cigarette, take a few drags, and blow the smoke right in the kid's face. And one detective says softly in a thick Irish brogue, "Look, lad, you came in here with two things: a lot of information and your good looks. You can't leave with both."

The kid talked.

AND HE WONDERS WHY HE NEVER MADE DETECTIVE

We worked in the Sixth Precinct in Greenwich Village, which is predominantly gay. That didn't bother 99 percent of the cops who worked there. Most of us couldn't care less what you do in your own time. We figure as long as you aren't shooting at us, we basically like ya. This Sergeant Finn who got transferred there, though, was a bit of a homophobe and just real uncomfortable around gay people. So like any good cops would do, we had to bust his chops about it. I put a rainbow flag sticker [a symbol of gay pride] on the rear bumper of his personal car. For months this dummy was getting flowers and phone numbers left on his car, and he kept coming to work asking, "Why do men keep hitting on me?"

Certainly not because of his intellect.

WARNING: SHUT UP!

In the '70s, my partner, Dougie O'Brien, was a tough old throwback of a cop, and he showed it one night when we were in the projects headed to an aided case on some nonviolent call. The elevator was out (gee, what a shock), so we had to take the stairs. Well, lucky us. In the staircase, we stumble upon a gun buy. There were two of them and two of us, but we were all so stunned to see each other that no words were exchanged. Everybody just reacted. One of them had an automatic weapon and wheeled around to fire on us, but we shot first, and the mutt went down. Holding his leg up by his groin where the bullet entered, he starts whining, "Man, you guys are supposed to give me a warning to drop my gun! You didn't give me no warning!"

Dougie starts cuffing the guy and yells at him, *"No warning?!* You want a warning? I'll give ya a f——n' warning. I'm warning you to shut the f——k up before I shoot you in the other leg!"

HER HUSBAND WON'T MIND

I used to work with this one female cop, Gina Scarda. She retired a sergeant and is now doing stand-up comedy all around the country about her experiences on the NYPD. Well, Gina is beautiful, with a body that could stop traffic. So what does the NYPD do with a woman who looks like that? They make her an undercover hooker. When I asked her if she minded doing that type of work, she told me, "Nah. I already had all the outfits, so I might as well put them to use."

Then she told me her captain asked her, "Is this going to cause any problems at home? Will your husband mind if you do this type of undercover work?"

Gina said, "Are you kidding? How do you I think met him? I still refer to him as Client Number Nine."

ONE OF US NOW

When rookies first get assigned out of the academy to a command, most veteran guys don't talk to them for a while. It's because we just want to see what kind of people they are and what kind of cops. There is a lot at stake, and you want to make sure the rookies have the character it takes to be a stand-up guy or gal. There are lots of ways to test this, and one of them is by pulling a nice prank.

Anyway, one day me and my partner, Heffernen, are headed back to the station house, and we see this rookie on his foot post headed the same way. We stop and say, "Get in, kid, we'll give ya a lift back."

Poor kid gets in the backseat with no clue as to what we had in store for him. Indeed, he thinks that now he is one of the guys.

So we head over to the car wash to put our plan into action. First, we roll down the rear windows and put them in lock position, along with the car door locks [in patrol cars, all locks are controlled up front]. Now the kid, about to go through the car wash, says, "Hey, guys, I can't get the windows up. Hey, guys?"

Heff says, "Look, rook. You're brand-new and we gotta make sure you're not a dirty cop. Ha ha ha." Then, with our front windows nice and tightly closed, we drive through the car wash, and he's getting blasted with water.

The whole way back we are laughing, but the kid doesn't say a word. When we get back to the station house, the DO [desk officer] asks the rookie, who is dripping wet, what the hell happened.

He says, "Well, sir, um—it's hot out there, and I have a glandular problem. I sweat a lot."

NOT TOO SERIOUS A CAESAR

One day, me and my partner, Mike Brook, are by the
United Nations, and we get waved down by a UN guard. He
tells us a man is having an epileptic seizure. We call
for an ambulance and just comfort him until it arrives
because with a seizure, there's not much you can do.
Just make sure they don't bang their head or bite their
tongue. So this tourist from the South thinks we're not
doing enough for the guy and starts yelling at us in his
thick southern accent: "Do somethin'! That boy be havin'
a Caesar!"

Brook looks up at him and says, "Really? A Caesar?
Would that be salad or palace?"

DIST ID	D.C. NO.	SECT.	DIST.	REPORT DATE
KCM006-A	59	HMR	980-09-12	4/5/2004

Whaddaya, Nuts?

We are riding on the Belt Parkway in Brooklyn when we see this guy swerving all over the road. So we stop him, and he reeks of booze. We get him out of the car and start to explain to him in detail the sobriety test that we are going to administer. You know, the usual. Walk the line, raise one foot, et cetera.

The drunk looks at us like we're crazy and says, "Whaddaya, nuts? I can't do that shit. I've been drinking all day!"

REPORT PREPARED BY

NO. 97253659

A RINGING IN HIS EARS

We had this lieutenant working midnights who was a real pain in the ass. He used to bust everybody's chops on everything, no matter how petty or stupid. So it got busy one night, and he didn't pick up the phone when a chief called. The chief chewed him out and threatened to transfer him if he didn't get his act together.

Now back in those pre–cell phone days, in the NYPD we had something called the "spin number." This was a code cops could use from a pay phone to call the station house for free if they needed to. This pain-in-the-ass lieutenant was on the desk again one night, so we gave the spin number out to all the homeless people in the precinct and told them to ask for the lieutenant because he would be treating everyone who called to food. The phone rang off the hook! Drove this lieutenant bonkers but he didn't dare not answer this time!

He was so busy answering the phone, we were also able to put liquid bubbles in his pipe.

WAKE-UP CALL

We had this real do-nothing female empty suit on the TS [telephone switchboard]. One night, per usual, she is sitting there talking to her girlfriends or her boyfriend or involved in some other personal phone call drama, the TS is lighting up like a Christmas tree, and she is not answering anything. It's also her job to screen people coming into the station house, and she isn't doing that, either. So me and a few of the guys in my squad get a few flares out of the backs of our patrol cars, put them together with duct tape, and tape them to an old alarm clock. We also talk the desk officer, who has a view of the front door, into becoming a coconspirator. We leave out the back, go around front, kick open the station house door, and toss the bomb into the precinct! We wait outside for about three minutes and can't believe nothing is happening. Suddenly, we see this empty suit burst out of the front door and race across the street covering her ears, waiting for an explosion. Do you know she never even said a word to the desk officer? But the stunt made us laugh, and at least it got her off the phone.

NOT SO COOL NOW, ARE YA?

Working in midtown you get all types of people committing crimes. You expect certain things, like a homeless guy stealing food or something. But when people do stuff just to be "cool" or to "rebel," it really pisses me off.

At any rate, one day we get this "holding one" [a shoplifter caught and detained by store security] at a big department store. So it's my post, and I show up expecting some poor person or junkie or something like that. To my surprise, I get this *very* well-dressed young college kid, who, it turns out, is an heir to a pretty famous family.

This kid is whining and complaining the whole way back to the station house. What a spoiled, look-down-at-you piece-of-garbage attitude the kid had. I am asking him basic questions for the 61 [complaint report] and he says with an attitude, "Hey! Is this going to take long? I have a few appointments I have to make. Let me just pay whatever this stupid little fine is and get out of here. Besides, there are real criminals out there you should be locking up!"

At this point I had just had it with him so I say, "I'm sorry, sir, are you a member of our rewards program? Maybe if you give me your NYPD rewards number we can check how many points you have accumulated and see if we can't get you out as fast as possible. Would you like to see a wine list while you wait? No? Good, then get in the f——n' cage!"

I threw him in a cell with one of the meanest, baddest-looking guys you could imagine—six-foot-five with scars and tattoos on his face, no neck, and all muscled up from pumping iron in jail.

"Sorry, sir. We don't have that single king-size bed overlooking the park like you requested. I hope this will do."

Then I take two steps to leave, and I stop and say to the six-five guy, "Listen, this is his first time here, so please don't be offended by him calling you ugly when he first walked in. Play nice."

That kid didn't move from the corner for three hours, until I processed his paperwork! I doubt he will be "rebelling" anymore.

ONE-LINERS

In gathering stories for this book, we received a number of funny one-liners. Here are some we particularly liked.

Rude passerby yells at a cop: "Yo, Five-oh! What's the fastest way to criminal court?"
Cop: "Hit me."

Perp's girlfriend: "Yo, Officer, my boyfriend got busted, and they told me they took him to the center library, where all the books are at."
Surprised cop: "You mean Central Booking?"
Perp's girlfriend: "Yeah, I think that's it."

An ex-cop told us that if he was on death row, he knew what he'd select as his last meal: "Soup--but I'd eat it with a fork."

A perp gets arrested and starts to have a seizure. His friends start yelling, "Yo, man, get my boy his peanut brittle for his seizer, Five-oh!"

Cop says, "You mean his phenobarbital medication?"

"Yeah, dat be it!"

OR SUMPIN'

Me and my partner were on patrol late one afternoon, and we roll up on two guys duking it out over some girl. We decide to bring them in because they went at it pretty good, and both were banged up good. Hence, we did a cross-complainant thing and figure we'll let the judge sort it out.

We take them back to the station house and run their IDs to make sure they don't pop on a warrant, and they both come back clean. We process them and give them a DAT, and I explain to one of these goofballs that it stands for desk appearance ticket, and it means he has to come back and go to court at a later date. He looks at me, glancing at the ticket. Then, as he's leaving, his girlfriend, who was waiting for him, asks, "What's that?"

He says, "I dunno. Da cop sed it's a disappearance ticket or sumpin'."

AHHH, THE GOOD OL' DAYS

When David Dinkins was the mayor (late '80s, early '90s), it was a pretty lawless New York City. People could have eighty suspensions on their license and not go to jail. When Rudy Giuliani came in, he changed that right away. One suspension and you were a keeper, which meant no DAT. You had to go to Central Booking and spend time in jail. It could be twenty-four to forty-eight hours before you were let out.

At any rate, we were doing a midnight tour one time, and we see this guy make an illegal U-turn. So we pull him over, and it's some fifty-year-old guy with thirty-six suspensions on his license. We have no choice but to arrest him.

He steps out of the car, and we cuff him. He is pretty apologetic, thinking he is just going to get a DAT and be on his way in two hours. So we explain the new rules to him and how we have to tow his car, which will cost him a few hundred bucks, and he has to be processed and go to Central Booking and see a judge. Since it is a Saturday night, he may not get out until Monday.

His whole demeanor changes. "Oh, man, this sucks!" he says. "Hey, Officers, have a heart. Can't you just toss me a beating like in the old days and let me go?"

I look at my partner, and we start laughing pretty hard at that and say, "When was the last time that happened? We don't do that anymore."

"*Ahhh*, back in the old days, you guys would slap me around a bit, throw my keys in the sewer, and let me walk home. Now you're taking me to jail for two days! Progress sucks. No wonder the city is broke!"

WELL, THAT'S DIFFERENT THEN

On a four-by-twelve tour we pull this teen over for a broken taillight. Turns out he has expired insurance. It's not a crime, but we can't let him drive the car, and it has to be towed. In order to tow it, we also have to search it. As we are searching it, the kid is pretty quiet and from under the seat we pull out about twenty dime bags of marijuana. *Now* it's a crime, so we cuff him, and he blurts out, "Hey, you can't arrest me for that!"

I say, "Yeah? Why not?"

With all seriousness he says, "'Cause that's for *smokin'*, not for *sellin'*!"

BY THE NUMBERS

When mob loan shark Ruby Stein was murdered by the
Westies gang, Stein was lured into an empty Manhattan
bar at ten o'clock in the morning and stabbed to death.
He was then cut up into a dozen pieces in a sink in the
back of the bar, and around two o'clock the pieces,
wrapped in plastic, were thrown into the East River.
A homicide detective succinctly described what happened:
"Ruby came into the bar at ten as one and left at two
as twelve."

NICE ASS!

M e and my partner, Mark, were riding in an anticrime car, which is an unmarked car made to look like a cab. It's actually a real cop car with lights and a siren on the inside, but nobody can see them from the outside.

It was a nice spring day in Manhattan, so we both had our windows down. Mark was driving, and I was in the passenger seat. We stopped at a red light, and I notice some construction guys doing work on the corner within earshot. So I nonchalantly say to Mark, "Is that the kid we're looking for on that robbery pattern?" He turns to look, and when he does, I yell toward the construction workers, real loud, "Hey, sexy! Nice ass!" And I drop down under the dash so nobody can see me.

The construction guys turn their heads and see Mark staring right at them. Now Mark is trying to explain it wasn't him, that there is some guy under the dashboard who yelled it, and that makes it ten times worse! They called him every name under the sun until the light turned green, and I was laughing my ass off!

EXPERIENCE IS THE BEST TEACHER

I was working in the 112 squad when this guy in his early thirties, an intellectual type, comes into the station house. His face is pretty battered, like he went a few rounds with a pretty good middleweight.

He says, "I was on my way home from Queens College, where I teach philosophy, when I came across this group of teenage girls. They asked me if I had the time. So when I looked at my watch, one of them hit me with something, and the others stomped on me and took my wallet."

A couple of us are listening to this guy in disbelief because of the damage to his face. Then the guy says, as he is touching his wounds, "I can't believe a woman could cause so much damage to a man."

That's when Detective Bernie Goldstein, who is in his late fifties, chimes in, "You obviously have never been married."

STRICT RULES OF HONOR

It was a relatively quiet Sunday afternoon in the Bushwick section of Brooklyn when me and my partner, Frankie Delgado, get a call about a family dispute. We head over to the job, and when we get there the dispute has now spilled over into the street. There are about fifteen people involved—men, women, and a few teens—but only two men are really fighting, and all the others are trying to keep them separated. One guy is armed with a broom handle, so me and Frankie get out and approach him. We say, "Whoa, whoa, whoa, slow down here, chief. What's the problem?"

He's calm with us, so I just take the handle out of his hands, and he starts pointing at the other guy and yells, "This punk ova here ain't no real man!"

I ask, "Is he related to you?" He tells me no, that the guy is his sister's boyfriend of the past ten years. So I ask him what happened to set this off.

"Here we are having a nice Sunday barbecue and some wine, and he hits my sister!"

I take a look at the lady he hit and don't see any damage, so I say, "OK, let's take it easy for now. Let us handle it and let's be grateful she isn't bleeding or badly bruised."

He shoots back, "Aw, damn! That ain't the point. That punk can't bruise a peach, but ain't *nobody* gonna hit my sistah unless he's *married* to her!"

PERP, A.K.A. CAR PAYMENT

New York City cops got paid like crap under Dinkins and Giuliani. When the city was doing well financially, we actually got 0 percent raises in some contracts, taking home less than $2,000 a month at *top pay*! In New York, that is barely above poverty level.

Because of that, overtime became a lifeline to survive financially. We had this guy, Billy Moran, who actually referred to his collared perps according to what bills were due, such as "refrigerator," "gas bill," "washing machine," et cetera.

So he locks up this low-level perp for drug possession. We are both back in the cell area doing paperwork when he gets up and calls to the perp in the cell, "Hey, Car Payment, c'mere. I have to print you."

DIST ID	D.C. NO.	SECT.	DIST.	REPORT DATE
KCM006-A	75	HMR	980-09-12	3/11/2006

Is All Right . . .

We get a call about a domestic disturbance on 138th and Willis Avenue, and when I get there, this one Hispanic guy is beating the daylights out of another one. Me and my partner break it up, and I say, "Whoa, Señor, slow down. What's the problem-- why the fisticuffs, *mi amigo*?"

With a heavy Hispanic accent he says, "I'm going to kill him, man. I just catched him laying my wife!"

We look at the other guy and ask if this is true.

Drunk, he replies, "Yeah, but is all right. She my seester!"

REPORT PREPARED BY

NO. 97253675

ALL I GOT LEFT!

It was a picture-perfect spring day one time in the 109th Precinct, and I was lucky enough to get a foot post. I liked foot posts on days like that, instead of being stuck in a radio car running from job to job. So I decided to take a stroll into the residential part of the community.

At one point, I pass this house where a woman in her sixties, dressed in a housecoat, is doing some light yard work. She stops me and says, "Officer, when are they gonna fix them streetlights? It's so dark up here at night because the trees block out all the moonlight—and it's dangerous."

"I don't know, ma'am. You would have to call Con Ed, but it's pretty quiet up in this part of the precinct—not much crime—so I wouldn't worry about it."

She says, "I know all about worrying. Just the other night I was almost raped."

"Almost raped? Did you report it?"

"No."

I reach for a complaint report in my memo book, and I ask her what happened.

She says, "I was taking out the garbage about eleven p.m., and these two young men were walking in the street leering at me, eyeballing me."

"Did they say anything or attack you?"

"Well, *no. But* it's so dark out here, and it was late. I was wearing my nightgown, and they *could* have just attacked me and held me hostage and ravished me and touched me all over. They could have practically made me their sex slave and done whatever they wanted to because it's so dark out here with these broken lights."

OK, I get it. I start to put my complaint report away, and I say, "Ma'am, I am sure it was nothing. I think you're watching a little too much TV, and you are letting your imagination get the best of you."

She nods, thinks about the reality *of what didn't happen*, and says, chuckling, "Listen, leave my imagination alone. At my age, it's all I got left."

WHAT'S UP?

W e were cruising in an RMP in Hell's Kitchen one time, when a call comes over the radio about a robbery two minutes in the past. We were about four blocks away, so we ask for a description of the suspect. Central comes back with black male, five feet ten inches tall, 170 pounds, white T-shirt, blue jeans, and a red St. Louis Cardinals baseball hat.

Just as it comes over the air, we see a guy fitting the description running our way, looking back over his shoulder in a nervous sort of way, and ducking behind parked cars. So we get out and stop him. Right away he starts going into his spiel: "I know why you stopping me—it's that state police racial profiling BS, that's what's up!"

I say, "I stopped you because you fit the description of a suspect we are looking for."

"You telling me I look like a suspect?"

My partner asks into the radio, "Central, please verify that description!"

Central responds, "Black male, five feet ten inches tall, one hundred and seventy pounds, white T-shirt, blue jeans, and red St. Louis Cardinals baseball hat."

"Oh, man, yeah, um—I just seen that guy. He's up the street, and I loved the hat so much, he gave it to me. He's your guy. Let's go get 'im!"

FUNNY TALES FROM 911 OPERATORS

Most of the time 911 operators get calls that are serious or unnecessary. But sometimes, they are just roaringly funny.

Dispatcher: "Nine-one-one, what is your emergency?"

Caller: "I heard what sounded like gunshots coming from the brown house on the corner."

Dispatcher: "Do you have an address?"

Caller: "No, I have on a blouse and slacks, why?"

Dispatcher: "Nine-one-one."

Caller: "Yeah, I'm having trouble breathing. I'm all out of breath. Darn—I think I'm going to pass out."

Dispatcher: "Sir, where are you calling from?"

Caller: "I'm at a pay phone. North and Foster."

Dispatcher: "Sir, an ambulance is on the way. Are you an asthmatic?"

Caller: "No."

Dispatcher: "What were you doing before you started having trouble breathing?"

Caller: "Running from the police."

PRETTY WOMAN?

One Saturday on a six-to-two night tour, I saw this car run a red light and weave all over the road. I hit the lights and pulled the car over. The driver was a female about twenty-five and had on this *real* skimpy outfit that should have come with a lamppost and a public defender. Turns out she wasn't drunk, but she was texting on her cell phone (which is a real pet peeve of mine because of all the accidents it causes) and had dropped the cell and tried to pick it up while she was still driving.

I started to tell her how dangerous texting while driving was, and she starts right in with "Don't you have anything better to do? There are real criminals out there, and you are wasting your time pulling me over. Do you know who I am?" Then she said she was some famous actress (I never heard of her) and needs to be on the set early and doesn't have time for this and blah blah blah.

I tell her, "Wait right here." I go back to my patrol car, run her information, and write her up. When I hand her two summonses, she barks out, "Hey, I thought cops don't give pretty women tickets?"

I said, "We don't." And I walked away.

DIST ID	D.C. NO.	SECT.	DIST.	REPORT DATE
KCM006-A	83	HMR	980-09-12	8/19/2008

Who Am I?

At night court, a guy stepped up in front of the judge, and the judge asked, "Are you the defendant?"

"No."

"Are you the complainant?"

"No."

"If you're not the complainant or the defendant, who are you?"

"I'm the guy who got arrested."

REPORT PREPARED BY

NO. 97253683

GOOD ENOUGH!

Former NYPD cop John DiResta, now a comedian, tells this story of when he was on a foot post in the subways back in the '80s. He saw this guy jump the turnstile to beat the fare. So John follows the guy and is going to write him a summons. He asks the guy for ID, but he has none. Now, you are supposed to bring a guy like that into the station house to ascertain his proper ID, but it's a real pain for everyone involved, and John recognizes the guy as a local lush—and harmless.

So John says to the guy, "Look, I'll tell you what I'll do. If you promise not to come around here again tonight, and you can answer a question correctly, I'll let you go."

The guy says, "Great. What's the question?"

John says, "Name three states not including New York or New Jersey."

Right away the guy says, "Florida." Then he takes a second and says, "Los Angeles."

John says, "That's a city, not a state, but I'll give it to ya."

Now the guy looks perplexed, and John looks at his watch and starts to pressure him like in a game show: "Quick, ten seconds or off to jail you go. Nine, eight, seven, hurry up, six, five, four, I am reaching for my cuffs, three, two, name another state."

The guy, all nervous, blurts out, "Upstate!"

"Good enough!"

UGLY IS UGLY

Back in the '70s, there was a rash of crimes involving shaking down patrons coming out of gay clubs. Well, this one openly gay guy comes into the station house with his shirt ripped, and you could tell he had been in a scuffle but not hurt too badly. There are a few of us at the front of the desk and we ask, "Can we help you, sir?"

He responds, all flustered, "I want to report a crime!"

"What happened?"

"Well, I was robbed coming out of a bar on West Fourth Street."

"What did the robber look like?"

The guy stops and thinks and says, "Well, it was pretty dark, but he was ugly!"

Obviously there isn't any box to check off on a police report for ugliness, so I had to ask, "Well, is that tall ugly or short ugly?"

He says, "What's the difference? When you're ugly, you're ugly!"

NO QUESTIONS ASKED

We had a DARE program [Drug Abuse Resistance Education] a few years back. The officer would go to a school many times during the year and give antidrug presentations to the kids and do stuff with them. I must say that the cop assigned to this detail was not the most, shall we say, aggressive type of person. I guess they chose him because he wouldn't intimidate the kids, but I didn't think of him as very bright, either.

At any rate, he had a huge stuffed bear he used for presentations to younger kids, but one day he made the mistake of leaving the bear in the front seat of his unlocked car, and the bear disappeared. The next day at roll call, a videotape mysteriously appeared in the squad room. It was played by the sergeant, and it showed two stuffed bears tied to a chair with gags over their mouths, and one of them was the officer's bear. Standing by were two hooded individuals holding a sign that read, "If you ever want to see your bear again, there better be two dozen doughnuts at roll call tomorrow morning!"

The next morning doughnuts showed up, and the bear was returned—no questions asked!

PERFECT TIMING

It was back in 1994 at the Forty-first Precinct and a couple of us decided to amuse ourselves at some rookie's expense. So we took some road flares, wrapped them with black electrical tape and a telephone cord, and attached them to a beeper. In those days everyone had beepers, not cell phones.

As I worked the desk, I pretended to field a call about some wack-a-doo who wanted to blow up the precinct. Then I told the rookie on station house security duty to do his job and check around outside. In those days, you could always count on one disgruntled customer a week threatening to blow something up. So it was pretty routine, and 99 percent of the time, it amounted to nothing.

We were watching the rookie on the monitors, and as he started in the direction of the garbage can where we had put the fake bomb, we called the beeper.

It was perfect timing! Just as he got to the package, it started to beep. Well, this kid comes running through the back door of the precinct screaming, "There's a bomb! Holy shit, there's a f——ng bomb!" He kept on going right out the front door without even slowing down.

About a minute or two later, he slowly walked back in to see why we did not evacuate, only to find everyone laughing our asses off and mimicking him in a feminine voice, "There's a bomb, there's a bomb! Run for the hills."

TRAPPED WITH MICKEY

Now, cops don't always get along well with attorneys. For the most part, we don't think they are ethical, and many (not all) try to build a career by taking down cops on the stand. So just to prove the point of how greedy and unethical we thought many of these folks are, we caught a large mouse in the courthouse, put it in a box, and gift wrapped it. We placed the box on a bench in the public hallway and waited. Wouldn't you know it, the one honest lawyer in the courthouse that day picked it up and turned it in to us! Ugh. So we changed the location and put it on the ledge in a public telephone booth.

Within a minute, we had a bite. A female attorney entered the booth, saw the "gift," and motioned for her friend to come into the booth, and they closed the door. They look around to see if anybody saw what they did, and when they thought nobody was looking, they opened the box, Mickey jumped out, and they start screaming! They tried to get out of the booth but couldn't open the door because it folded in, and their buttocks were a little overstuffed. They were trapped with Mickey, the booth was rocking, and they almost killed each other trying to get out. We almost died laughing!

YOU'D SWEAT, TOO

In the late '30s, the NYPD mounted police dressed heavily, even in summer, and it wasn't long before they would be sweating freely.

One day when it was particularly hot out, a mounted cop began sweating almost instantly. Mounted cops always attract their share of the fair sex, and this was a good-looking guy who attracted lots of women. His only problem, though, was that he was nervous around pretty women, and this one day, he was approached by one who was just gorgeous.

When she got close, she looked up at him and said, "You're sweating a lot."

Trying to be cool, he blurted out, "You'd be sweating, too, if you had this much meat between your legs."

The woman let out with a high-pitched cackle that seemed to last forever, and the cop just sat there, sweat rolling off him and his stomach curdling.

PEEP SHOW

One day in Narco I see one of the old-timers looking out a window with binoculars, and I wonder what the hell he's doing. Suddenly he half gasps to one of the newbies on the squad, "Oh, no! I can't believe it. Two girls are having sex in a car!"

All excited, the newbie runs over.

"Let me see, let me see."

The old-timer passes the binocs to another guy who has been in the unit awhile, and when he uses them he says, "Oh, my God, I've never seen anything like that before!"

Now the newbie is grabbing at the binocs, so we let him have them. Looking hard through the binocs, he says, "I don't see anything."

We tell him it's that gray car down there, and he looks again and says, "I still don't see anything."

One of us says, "Maybe you need to focus the binocs." He does and says, "I don't see anything."

Finally, he takes the binocs away from his eyes, and he looks like a raccoon. The eye portions of the binocs were smeared with Xerox tint. He went about thirty minutes before he passed a mirror and noticed it. We were laughing the whole time!

IT'S A WONDER HE CAN SEE AT ALL

My partner and I were on a day tour doing a routine patrol when we see the car in front of us go right through a stop sign. I decide to follow him while my partner runs his plate. The car comes back clean, but he runs another stop sign and makes an illegal U-turn. We pull the car over, and the driver is a male in his seventies. He has this big smile on his face. I ask him for his license and insurance card.

He gives them to me and asks, "What did I do, Officer?"

I said, "You went through two stop signs and made an illegal U-turn."

He asks, real innocent like, "What signs?"

"The signs back there. How could you miss them?"

He looks at me kind of sheepishly and says, "Well, to tell you the truth, I don't see so good. The doctor says I got Cadillacs in my eyes."

IT'S WHAT WE DO

On late tours, my partner, Joey, would always try to get some rest on slow nights when we ride on patrol. Joey snores like a jet engine, so one night I was a little bored driving this two-hundred-pound snore machine around, and I decide to have some fun with him. Why? Because we're cops, and that's what we do. So I gun the gas, get the RMP up over 100 mph, and stick the radar set out the window to lock in the speed. Then I spot this guy waiting for a tow truck in his disabled vehicle on the shoulder of the Belt Parkway in Brooklyn, and I pull to a stop behind him. I smack my partner and tell him, "Hey, I just chased this guy for over a mile. Will ya wake up and do some work tonight? It's your turn to write him."

He wipes his eyes, gets a look at the radar set, and sees the speed. He gets out and starts yelling at this poor guy—who simply can't get his car started—that he was stopped for doing 100 in a 50 mph zone. "Hey, jerk-off, you know we chased you for over a mile?"

The guy looks at Joey like he's crazy and snaps back, "Well you must have been chasing me on foot, Columbo, because I have been stuck here for twenty minutes!" After watching Joey's face and the guy's face, with both of them staring at each other in disbelief, I was hysterical. I had to apologize to the guy and tell him it must have been a car that looked just liked his.

PAYBACK

I was being harassed for weeks by my fellow officers for my inability to take prints well. As a former jailer, my partner, Mark, was especially picky about it. One evening when I arrested a Hispanic male who spoke no English, I decided to get even with Mark.

I understood some Spanish, so I explained to the arrestee that he was going to be printed by Mark, and I told him something else in Spanish as well. Then I left the area.

A few minutes later Mark came into the office where I was sitting, and he asked if I'd explained to this guy what was happening with the printing. "Of course," I said, but Mark scratched his head and told me the guy was being very uncooperative, even treating Mark as if he had bubonic plague.

I went back into the booking area and told the guy about the printing again, and I watched as Mark successfully printed him, though the guy still had this standoffish, even scared, attitude.

Next, Mark asked if I wanted to transport the arrestee to the jail. I said I would do it, but then asked the arrestee if he wanted to ride in the patrol car with Mark. The arrestee went a little nuts, shaking his head wildly and spouting something in

Spanish, which I barely understood and about which Mark had no clue. This irked Mark to the point that he changed his mind and insisted on taking the guy to the jail, and I let him.

Upon his return, Mark came into the office and was miffed. On the way to the jail, the guy's crazy attitude toward him had continued. I nodded and walked outside with Mark and then got into my patrol car. I started the engine, rolled down the window, and asked Mark if he'd ever considered taking Spanish lessons. Of course he answered, "No." Then, putting the car in drive and getting ready for a quick getaway, I told him that he probably should because I had told the arrestee in Spanish that Mark was a good officer, the only problem being that he liked boys, especially dark-skinned Latino boys with black hair and brown eyes! Then I blasted away, laughing so hard I almost lost control of the car.

WHAT'S THAT ON YOUR HEAD?

In the late '80s, I worked with this really hot Italian sergeant named Gina, a Marisa Tomei type. She was *very* sharp-tongued and witty and had her twenty years in. She could have retired but you would never know it, since she didn't look a day over thirty. Having her twenty in protected her, because bosses tended not to mess with someone they knew could just throw their retirement papers in on the spot.

Now, Gina did have run-ins with one boss, a jerk-off captain in Manhattan North Inspections, a real ball breaker. It had gone on for twenty years. Maybe he was pissed at her, because he was always flirting with her but she always quickly rebuffed him, and maybe he was self-conscious about his toupee, which was the worst I ever saw.

Anyway, this one time he sees her at a detail by Columbus Circle and spots her wearing earrings, which technically are not allowed when an officer is in uniform. He barks at her, "Officer, what are those adornments in your ears?"

Without even missing a beat, she nods and shoots back, "What's that adornment on your head?"

He ducked his head and just slithered away.

DIST ID	D.C. NO.	SECT.	DIST.	REPORT DATE
KCM006-A	100	HMR	980-09-12	10/27/2009

Not His Strong Suit

We get a call one night about some kid breaking into cars on a certain street. So we go there, cutting the lights just when we arrive. We see the kid, and I hop out of the car and cover one end of the block. My partner takes the car and circles around and blocks the other end.

Well, somehow this mutt looks up, bolts toward me, and we collide. We wrestle a bit, but I finally get the cuffs on him. I guess in the mayhem I may have put them on a little too tight because the kid starts whining, "Yo, Five-oh, yo, these cuffs are so tight my hands are going brain-dead!"

In that instant, I knew why he became a thief and not a physical therapist: Clearly, anatomy was not his strong suit.

REPORT PREPARED BY *[signature]*   NO. 4830001100

KARATE KID HE AIN'T

Four years ago, my partner and I get a call about a violent nutcase strung out on crack cocaine high on the roof of an apartment building. We respond, and there is this 250-pound monster of a guy, armed with a set of nunchucks [a Chinese weapon consisting of two pipes connected by a short chain], screaming that he sees ninjas all around, and they are attacking him. He looks like a kung fu grandmaster, whirling these nunchucks every which way, and none of us want to go anywhere near him.

We sort of contain him, but do nothing, just wait for an ESU [emergency service unit] to show up.

Then it happens. He's whirling these nunchucks between his legs and accidentally whacks himself square in the balls, so hard it sounds like a balloon popped!

He goes down on his knees and starts crying like a little girl as he uses his hands to cup his balls, trying to make the pain go away. Now we can go cuff him, and my partner says to him, "Well, I guess it's safe to say you won't be getting that job as Chuck Norris's stunt double."

DIST ID	D.C. NO.	SECT.	DIST.	REPORT DATE
KCM006-A	102	HMR	980-09-12	10/12/2009

An Unusual Diagram

I was investigating the theft of some bicycles and had apprehended a suspect. He was a juvenile and could not be interviewed until his mother arrived. When she did, she was very angry and began to name a lot of other suspects. We asked where the suspects lived, and the woman asked me for a piece of paper, saying, "Let me draw you a diaphragm."

It took all the strength I could muster not to burst out laughing. I didn't have the heart to correct her, so I just gave her the paper and thanked her for her diaphragm.

REPORT PREPARED BY *John Law*

NO. 4830001102

HOW DARE HE!

A woman had stabbed her husband with a kitchen knife. There was blood all over the floor—he was really cut. So we stuck him in the wagon and shot him down to the hospital, but he was DOA.

We called the sergeant down to the hospital, which was the procedure at the time. He said, "Go back and lock her up."

We went back to the house and told her, "You're going to have to come with us."

"Why?" she asked.

"Your husband died."

"What?"

"Your husband is dead, and you're under arrest."

"That motherf——r died? Damn! I stabbed him worse than that before and it never killed him! *Now* he dies?!"

WE LIKED YOU BETTER
THE OTHER WAY

B ack in the '70s, if you were a gay cop you probably weren't as accepted as you might be today. In fact, you would try to hide it for fear of possible retribution. I was pretty open-minded, but my partner, Oscar, was a good guy if kind of like Archie Bunker when it came to that social stuff. One night when we were patrolling the West Village, we get a complaint from some people that a wild, boisterous party is being held in an apartment on West Fourth Street.

We respond and knock on the door. It opens up, and inside are a bunch of gay guys dancing and making out and so forth.

This one young, good-looking guy comes forward and says, "I'm an interior decorator, this is my apartment, and I apologize for the loudness. We'll tone it down."

"OK," I say. "You better or we'll have to issue a summons."

Then we're on our way back to patrol, and we get another complaint about noise coming from the same apartment.

We go back, and the same young guy answers the knock.

I say, "Look, pal, we were here once, and I'm not coming back again. So clear these people out because you can't keep the noise down!"

He apologizes up and down for the disturbance, and then steps out into the hall, closing the door behind him.

He says softly, "Look, I'm on the job."

"You're a cop? Got any ID?"

From an inside pocket he pulls out his police ID, and he is a cop. I hand him back his ID and Oscar says, "Geez, I liked you better as an interior decorator."

DON'T JUDGE A BOOK BY ITS COVER

We were on patrol one night on a four-by-twelve during the holidays when we see this car weaving all over the road. We pull it over, and the driver is a woman who is attractive but has a very puritanical appearance about her, almost like a librarian. Her hair is up in a bun, and she is wearing conservative glasses, with her blouse buttoned up to her neck. She attempts to explain that she was on her way home from her office holiday party, but it was obvious she had had way too much to drink. My partner and I were feeling real bad about having to arrest her, but we did. One look at her, and you would guess she had never been in trouble a day in her life. We explained she was being arrested for DWI, and she willingly put her hands behind her back to be cuffed. As I am putting the cuffs on her, she lets out a very loud groan and says, "Oh, my God."

I didn't want to hurt her, so I asked, "What's the matter, ma'am? Are the cuffs too tight?"

She said, "No, not at all. It's just that they make me *really* horny!"

ALL MY BEST

It's different today, but back when I was on the job, a lot of cops got a lot of freebies, including meals, on the tin. My partner was, pure and simple, a greedy bastard, and whenever we went into this small Greek restaurant off Fordham Road, I would pay for myself--the restaurant barely got by--but my partner never failed to do the old trick of handing the owner a ten-dollar bill, say, to pay for his four-dollar check and then getting his change--ten dollars.

At one point my partner's wife became pregnant, and every time he came into the restaurant, the owner would smile broadly and say something in Greek. We asked him what he was saying, and he said, "It's a good thing--a blessing in Greek meaning good luck with the new baby." I never forgot the phrase even though I didn't know what it meant exactly, and one day I got a new partner who was fluent in Greek. I asked him what it meant, and he laughed out loud. It meant "I sincerely hope your baby is born without legs."

GOOD NEWS FOR A MORNING LOON

It was one of those great spring days that make you love being a cop in NYC. It was kind of slow around 8:30 a.m. in midtown, and everyone was scurrying to work. My partner, Steve, and I were in an RMP and decided to park the car, roll down the windows, and just people watch. Now, when you do that, you run the risk of having some EDP [emotionally disturbed person] come up to you and start a conversation about nothing. Sure enough, within thirty seconds some old guy comes up to my window and says, "I ain't goin'!"

So I say, very nonchalantly, "OK, don't go. I wouldn't go, either."

Steve chimes in, "You couldn't pay me to go."

We have no idea what this guy is even talking about, but we figure he's just another morning loon.

The guy answers back, "They can't make me go. I am against it! I've been against it from the beginning."

Then he starts chanting, "Hell no, we won't go. Hell no, we won't go!"

Now he has my curiosity up, so I ask him, "Exactly where is it that you won't go?"

He hands me a leaflet from a U.S. Army recruiting station and says, "They want to draft me but I ain't goin'."

I start to chuckle a little bit because this guy is like sixty-five years old. I hand the pamphlet over to Steve. He looks at it, leans across to my window, and says, "Don't worry, old-timer. You're safe. You don't have to go. It just came over the air—Lee surrendered to Grant. The war's over. Go home!"

The guy gave us a surprised look and said, "Really? Thanks, Officer, that's great. You made my day!"

BE ON THE LOOKOUT FOR MR. SNUFFLEUPAGUS

A call comes over the radio one morning about a guy who has some illegal pets in his backyard. You need a permit for certain pets, and the property has to be zoned for it. He didn't have anything dangerous like tigers, but he did have a lot of farm animals. It was not a dangerous job, so we let a rookie pick it up. All of sudden we hear a panic call come over the radio: "Chasing big bird!"

It turns out as soon as the rookie went in the backyard, an ostrich ran out and down the street. The rookie started a foot pursuit, running and trying to talk into the radio, but his hand kept coming off the transmit button, and we only got part of his message. He tried to say, "An ostrich got loose. I am chasing a big bird!" But we only got "'Chasing big bird!"

So I had to answer back over the air, "OK, I'll be there in a minute, as soon as I finish cuffing the Cookie Monster!"

OY VEY

I worked with this tough cop we nicknamed Oy Vey. People did not want to mess with him. He weighed about 260 and had been a weightlifter since the age of twelve. He had a fifty-eight-inch chest, a thirty-one-inch waist, twenty-two-inch arms, and eighteen-inch calves. It was like having a lion on a leash.

There were three jokes in the precinct about him:

First, it was rumored that he was the only guy in the mounted unit who could do crowd control without a horse.

Second, they said his intelligence was in inverse proportion to his size.

And the third was that before you told Oy Vey the second joke—have your will drawn up.

We went to a family dispute with a big guy who was beating up his girlfriend and did not want to go peacefully. He starts yelling, "I ain't going anywhere! No way you pigs are taking me. C'mon, I'm ready for y'all!"

And then he sees Oy Vey step out of the car.

So I say to the guy, "Look, you're coming with us. The only question is whether you're gonna be vertical or horizontal."

COMPLAINT OR INCIDENT REPORT

DIST ID	D.C. NO.	SECT.		DIST.	REPORT DATE
KCM006-A	112		HMR	980-09-12	01/03/1996

S . . . M . . . One

My name is Smith. Once I got a call about a
family dispute, and the whole family is intox
[intoxicated]. They are a mess and just want to
argue with everyone. They don't even remember
what they are arguing about. One of the females
doesn't like how we're handling the job and says,
"I wanna make a civilian complaint, I'm callin'
IAD [Internal Affairs Division]!" She dials random
numbers and says, "Yeah, I wanna make a complaint.
His name? Hold on, I'll spell it."

   She squints to look at my nameplate and says,
"S . . . M . . . one." At that point we all started
laughing.

REPORT PREPARED BY *(signature)*   NO. 4830001112

"OH, STEWARDESS, I SPEAK JIVE"

I'm from a small town in upstate New York, so the thought of being a cop in a big city excited me. I joined the NYPD. However, I was very naive when I first started; I didn't speak a word of "urban." First week on patrol, we get a call about a dispute in the hood. We pull up and this twenty-something male is bleeding from the mouth. I am trying to act like a cool veteran cop, so I go up to the guy and ask, "OK, what happened?"

He says, "That trifling ho hit me in the grill with a slide."

I was like, "What the hell did he just say and what could that possibly mean?" My partner, who had grown up in the city and was way more hip than I was, took mercy on me and saw that I was lost and tells me, "In English it means 'My girlfriend got upset and hit me in the mouth with an iron.'"

I figured working in the city would be a challenge, but I didn't know you had to learn a foreign language.

NASTY STUFF

Back in the '70s, when you could get away with a lot more "street justice" than you can now, we had our own way of dealing with certain people and situations. There was this one guy who was peddling dope to kids, but he was smart enough to never have anything on him. He would just "employ" minors to do the deliveries. If a minor got caught, it was a slap on the wrist, and they were left in their parents' custody—parents who were usually addicts themselves.

So this guy would really piss us off, and we hassled him every day. On this particular day, I pull him over, and he stops his car in front of a fire hydrant. I write him a ticket for every violation I can think of, including one for being parked in front of the pump.

He's *fuming*! As I head back to my car he yells, "Man you are a real motherf——r!"

I open my door, and before I get in, I yell back, "You're right, I am. But tell your mother to double her price to a buck, and I won't f——k her no more."

WELCOME TO THE NEW YORK CITY POLICE DEPARTMENT

It was in East New York, which is a really tough area of Brooklyn. I was only on the job for about a week, and I was walking down the block and noticed this dirty, disheveled, really heavyset woman standing on her stoop staring at me. I stopped and asked her if everything was all right. She smiles and says, "Ooooh, I like a man in uniform." Then she turns halfway around, bends over a bit, and lifts up her skirt and asks, "You want to have some fun today? It's yours for ten dollars."

After trying not to throw up in my mouth, I answered, "I'm only a rookie. We don't make much money. I only have a dollar to my name, so have a good day."

I start to leave and she says, "Wait."

I stop, and as I did, she slaps her backside. "I'll take it. You can owe me the rest. I'm the original layaway, baby!"

THE ONLY THING GOLDEN . . .

Let's face it, old people are not good drivers. Statistics show this all the time, and I see it on the job every day—accident after accident, violation after violation.

Sometimes you give 'em a warning and let 'em go. Or sometimes, if they are a real danger to someone, you have to give 'em a ticket.

I let one lady off because of a comment she made.

She had run right through a stop sign, and I pulled her over.

She was your typical gray-haired portly grandmother type. No way I was going to give her a ticket, but I did give her a gentle lecture about being careful and how I wouldn't want to see her get hurt or hurt anybody else. Then I finished it off with a statement that these were her golden years, and she should try to live them wisely.

Well, she looks at me like I don't have a clue about life and says, "Honey, the only thing golden about my golden years is my urine."

CONCEALED WEAPON

Me and my partner, Raymo, get a call one day about a 10-10 [possible crime] from a four-story walk-up in the West Village. So we head over there, hit the buzzer, and a neighbor lets us in. We can hear the ruckus as soon as we get in the building. Screaming, cursing, threats—you'd think someone was trying to murder someone. As we are running up the stairs, the neighbors tell us this goes on all the time.

We get up the stairs, and two good-looking women are screaming in the hallway, wrestling around, pulling at each other's hair, really going at it. Me and Raymo each grab one and separate them and tell them, "Take it easy and try to remember, we're all ladies here! Now, *what* could have started this?"

Well, the blonde starts to tell us she lives here with her boyfriend and the brunette was told to stay away but keeps coming around. The brunette shoots back, "Bats [that was the boyfriend's name] doesn't want to be with you anymore. He wants me, and that's where he was last night, at my house." And on and on. As this is going on, we hear someone walking up the stairs yelling, "What the hell is going on?"

The blonde says, "Good. Bats is here. *He* will set you straight!"

Now, since these girls were pretty good-looking and can get any guy they want, I was thinking this guy must be really good-looking, too, or rich to have these girls this worked up. Then up from the stairs and into the hallway steps Bats, and he's a midget! Nothing wrong with that, but it just took me by surprise. He is actually pretty muscular, and I guess he just got back from the gym because he was wearing sweats and a tank top. Bats goes *nuts* and starts ranting, "I am so sick of all you girls always causing drama!" He points to the brunette. "You! Leave and don't ever show up uninvited!" Then he looks at the blonde and says, "And you get back in the apartment. I will deal with you in a bit!"

Now I am thinking, "Did he just say, 'all you girls'? How many does this guy have?"

So now it's just me, Raymo, and Bats in the hallway. Bats is very apologetic, saying sorry to cause us any trouble. Raymo says, "No problem. Yeah, girlfriends can drive you crazy. I guess that's why they call you Bats."

He says, "No, that's not it."

So I ask, "Why, then?"

Bats looks around to make sure it's just us three, and he pulls down his sweats and says, "'Bats' is short for baseball bat." I swear the thing almost hit the floor and broke the tiles! Me and Raymo just look at each other in amazement.

Raymo says, "Geez, you're a freakin' tripod!" And we literally start applauding, saying, "Good for you!"

As we are walking down the stairs, Raymo asks, "Did you see that thing?"

"See it? Are you kidding? I was gonna lock him up for carrying a concealed weapon!"

GOT HIM HOT IN THE WRONG WAY

I got called to a nursing home for a dispute between family members and the staff on how their mother was being treated. No big job, and it all worked out. But as we were leaving, I feel someone tug on my arm from behind. I turn around, and it's this guy in his seventies. He is wearing nothing except a Brooklyn Dodgers baseball cap, white Fruit of the Loom underwear, and black dress socks. "Officer, thank God you're here! I want to report a rape."

Well, that has my attention because you do hear horror stories on how some old people are abused in some of these nursing homes. So I ask, "You saw someone being raped?"

"No, me."

"You were raped?"

"Well, no, but sexually harassed."

Now I realize the guy is completely shot, but I ask anyway: "What happened? Why are you half-naked?"

"Well, the Jamaican nurse really loves my body, so she turns up the heat all the way in my room, so I have to walk around naked."

"The nurse does this?"

"Yeah, but it's not the heat, it's the humidity that drives me nuts. Then when I undress, she hides my clothes so I stay naked."

"Well, maybe she likes you. Maybe you should ask her out, maybe marry her."

"Marry her! Why the hell would I do that? She's Jamaican, and I can't understand a word she says! She practices that voodoo and tries to put me under a spell." Then he pauses for a second and says, "I'll sleep with her, but I won't marry her!"

"DON' PAY HIM NO MIND"

A deputy was patrolling a dark rural road when he observed a car running without taillights. It was late, and the deputy was tired; plus, it was the end of his shift. He didn't want to deal with it, but he knew he had to do something. Then he saw a driveway intersecting with the road he and the other car were on and saw the car slowing down. He figured if the driver lived there, he'd be off the road, in no danger to himself or others, and the deputy could avoid a lot of paperwork. Still, he wanted to give him a verbal warning, so he pulled the car over within a few yards of the country driveway.

As the deputy walked toward the car, he saw the driver stick his old grizzled head out the window. Before the deputy could say anything, the driver said, "Swear ta God, Office, I'm goin' down to the courthouse first thing in the morning and get my driver's license."

By this time, the deputy was even with the open driver's window. A woman in the passenger seat as old as the driver leaned toward him and yelled, "Don' pay him no mind. He jus' drunk."

The deputy was very late getting home.

COMPLAINT OR INCIDENT REPORT

DIST. ID	D.C. NO.	SECT.		DIST.	REPORT DATE
KCM006-A	123		HMR	980-09-12	5/29/2010

Claude the Cool

I was a Virginia Beach police officer from 1974 to 1984. On a stifling hot summer day in the height of tourist season, we received a call about a huge traffic backup at a major intersection in the resort area near the oceanfront. Upon arrival, we found Claude Vincent, one of our well-known street people, causing the chaos. He was directing traffic at the intersection--which was already controlled by a properly functioning traffic light--waving his arms frantically, yelling directions to drivers, and staying cool by being dressed only in a chrome army helmet, black combat boots, and a jock strap.

REPORT PREPARED BY

NO. 972536123

TOO BAD IT WASN'T
AN ELEPHANT

In Smithtown, New York, there is an impressive bronze bull—it weighs five tons, it's nine feet high and fourteen feet long, and it sits on a six-foot pedestal. In the spring of each year, vandals would paint the bull's hanging oversized testicles bright red, much to the embarrassment of the police, who, try as they may, could not find out who the perps were. Then one day a young cop named Howard McCormick, determined to find out who was doing it, surveilled a parking lot where there had been some robberies and saw three teenagers get out of a car and put something in the back of a pickup truck. McCormick went over and confronted them. He asked for license and registration, then went to see what they had put in the truck. He discovered a can of red paint. The kids quickly wilted and admitted to painting the bull's testicles.

Back at the station house, McCormick's commanding officer was ecstatic and immediately promoted him to a "steady seat" in a radio car, relieving him of his foot post duty.

One of his fellow cops later said, "Too bad it wasn't a statue of an elephant. They would have made McCormick commissioner!"

DIST ID	D.C. NO.	SECT.		DIST.	REPORT DATE
KCM006-A	126	HMR		980-09-12	10/02/2002

Dunce Car

I was on my foot post when, as usual, my boss, Sergeant Atkins, drove up to give me a scratch in my memo book. But I had to turn away so he couldn't see me laugh. Someone had placed a two-foot-high orange traffic cone over the red dome light on the roof of the car, and it looked like a dunce cap.

When he left, I really burst out laughing and found out later that he drove around another two hours with none of the cops who saw it alerting him. When he finally got out of the car, he saw it and laughed as hard as anybody.

REPORT PREPARED BY _John Law_   NO. 4830001126

"OK, SMART-ASS, READ 'EM . . ."

Back when I was working in Georgia near the Alabama state line, we often had to interface with cops from our neighboring state. There was always a friendly rivalry among us. One of our favorite shots at the 'Bama boys was to tell them about the time an Alabama trooper pulled a guy over.

"Lemme see yer license and registration, sir," the 'Bama trooper said in his most serious tone.

The nervous driver produced both documents and handed them over.

The trooper held them out in front of his face, scowled, and turned them sideways and upside down as if he didn't know what they were. Growling, he handed them back to the driver and said, "OK, smart-ass. Read 'em to me."

IT MIGHT BE A GOOD IDEA TO UPDATE YOUR WARDROBE

My partner and I were assigned to take a mentally disturbed fiftyish woman to Central Islip State Hospital and, following procedure, we were accompanied by a police matron named Fran. When we got to the hospital, we went through the committal procedure, and then my partner and I stepped outside to take a little break while Fran stayed with the EDP until attendants could take her to the ward.

When we came back inside, we immediately became aware of loud yelling at the end of the corridor. It was Fran, yelling at two big white-uniformed guys manhandling her. "Let me go, you assholes. Let me go! I'm a police matron. My freakin' badge is in my pocket!" But looking at her badge wasn't their job, so they didn't.

Finally, they let her go when we confirmed her ID. They said that when they arrived to take the EDP inside, the frumpily dressed Fran was sitting alone, her head slumped, looking exactly like any other mental patient might look. Fran admitted she had fallen asleep while she waited with the woman, and she was the only person on the bench when the attendants came out to get her.

But where was the EDP now? A frantic search ensued, and we found her having a cup of coffee in the cafeteria.

On the way back to the station, we almost made it without laughing, until my partner said, "Don't worry, Fran. We'll be sure to visit you regularly."

"PLEASE TELL ME IT'S SO"

We had a lot of problems in Portsmouth with what we called "he-she" prostitutes, men dressed up to look like attractive women, and we were looking to break it all up. We figured the best way to do it was to get an undercover agent in there, and Melvin Dunn, who was quite a character, volunteered.

We wired him for sound, but that was hardly the only thing we did. We transformed Melvin into a beautiful woman, complete with falsies, a tight red dress, stockings, makeup, false nails, and a wig. He looked perfect, sexy as all hell, and when he walked he wagged his butt with the best.

The first night on the street he was out for a couple of hours, and he was walking down the street when we suddenly saw three women walking toward him. We heard him utter a few panicky four-letter words, which was unusual for Melvin because he was a religious guy. Turns out one of the women was his wife, and he had neglected to tell her he was going undercover.

Melvin had no place to hide. The only thing he could do was take a few short steps to a store window and stand in front of it as if he was very interested in the display. They almost passed by, but in the window reflection he saw his wife approach him, and she had a look of total terror and consternation on her face.

"Melvin Dunn? Is that you?"

He could not speak.

"Lord," she said, "please tell me you're doing this for the police."

THE PROOF IS IN THE POWDER

Early on in my career I had a partner who cheated on his wife, and occasionally he would make me a coconspirator. One time he asked me to pick him up at his house and drive him to a certain phone booth where he would be picked up by his girlfriend. When the date was over, she would drop him off at the same phone booth, and he would call me to pick him up and drop him home.

This I did, but before we got to his house, he asked me to stop at a grocery store that was nowhere close to his neighborhood. I was surprised when he came out of the store with a small bag of flour, which he promptly opened and started pouring all over himself—from his hair to his shoes. People were watching him as if he was nuts. Finally finished, he brushed off the excess and got in the car.

"What was that all about?" I asked.

"Oh," he said, "I told her that I was going to help a friend hang Sheetrock."

DIST ID	D.C. NO.	SECT.	DIST.	REPORT DATE
KCM006-A	133	HMR	980-09-12	9/12/2007

A Serious Malady

You hear some hilarious stuff on the job, and some of the funniest comes from kids. I once went to a house looking for a woman I needed some info from, and her six- or seven-year-old daughter answered the door.

"Hi. Where's your mommy?" I asked.

"She's at the hospital."

"Oh. What's she doing there?"

"She's having her independence removed."

REPORT PREPARED BY

NO. 972536133

EXIT LAUGHING

Death row cops get to hear some of the funniest lines—the last words of the condemned. Here are a few samples:

"Well, gentlemen, you are about to see a baked Appel."

—*George Appel, executed by electric chair on April 1, 1928*

"I guess nobody is going to call."

—*Earl Johnson, executed May 20, 1987*

"Yeah, I think I'd rather be fishing."

—*Jimmy Glass, executed June 12, 1987*

"Capital punishment-- them without the capital get the punishment."

—*John Spenkelink, executed May 25, 1979*

"You can be a king or a street sweeper,
but everyone dances with the Grim Reaper."
—*Robert Alton Harris, executed on April 21, 1992*

"How about this for a headline for
tomorrow's paper: 'French Fries.'"
—*James French, executed by electric chair on August 10, 1966*

FUNNY PRECINCT T-SHIRTS

The Seventy-fifth Precinct, in Brooklyn, has a Christmas shirt with the NYPD shield with a Santa cap on the front, and the back has Santa being mugged with his reindeers tied up. It says, "Season's beatings from East New York."

Back in the mid '80s, New York City was known (and kind of still is) for its large rat population and the huge rats in the subways. Transit had a T-shirt showing a cop riding a big rat, charging through the transit tunnels. It read, "Transit Mounted Patrol."

The Bronx Narcotics Division has a shirt with the words "All Sales Are Final."

TWO FROM IRELAND

*We don't exactly know where these two stories came from—
we've found them in a few places—but we think Ireland, where
the cops are called the Garda.*

A motorist received in the mail a photo of his car speeding
through an automated checkpoint on a highway in Ireland,
and an £80 speeding ticket was included. Being a wise guy, the
speeder sent the Garda a photo of the money to pay it. The
Garda responded with a photo of a set of handcuffs, and the
money was paid.

A young woman was pulled over for speeding in Dublin. A
traffic cop walked up to her car window, flipping open his
ticket book as he did. When he got to the car the young lady
said, "I bet you're going to sell me a ticket to the Garda Traffic
Department Ball?"

The cop immediately replied, "The Garda Traffic Department
don't have balls."

FUNNY COP LINGO

adiosis, state of. In Suffolk County, New York, this is the cops' way of describing someone who has just died or is about to.

bag bride. A prostitute who smokes crack cocaine.

blizzard. A cluster of traffic summonses issued to one driver all at once. Also called a "package" of summonses.

blue flu. A group of police officers feigning illness.

dinosaur. A cop who has been working on the police force for a long time, or an older officer who won't change his outmoded ways.

Dirty Harriet. In the Midwest, the female equivalent of Dirty Harry.

doing the Houdini. Getting rid of a murder victim's body by cutting it into multiple pieces and throwing the pieces into a large body of water.

donorcycle. This is mostly used by accident investigators in the Midwest. Because motorcycles are so hazardous to ride, many drivers end up donating their organs for medical use.

dry dive. Committing suicide by jumping. The term is particularly popular with Chicago cops.

fat pill. A buttered roll.

finger wave. The digital examination of a prison inmate's rectum in a search for contraband.

flute. A whiskey bottle hidden in a bag.

Henry Lee Lucas Memorial Highway. The name cops gave to the stretch of Interstate 10 that begins near Laredo, Texas, and ends at the Interstate 75 exit to Gainesville, Florida. Along this road, serial killer Henry Lee Lucas was very active and dumped many bodies.

hook. Tow truck.

maggot. Term that New York City cops frequently use to describe a highly undesirable criminal.

make a canoe. An autopsy. At one point during the procedure, the body is hollowed out and resembles a canoe shape.

Mexican lightning. In California, it means arson for profit. The New York counterpart is "Jewish lightning."

mutt. Another popular term to describe really bad guys.

perp walk. The orchestrated showing of a suspect or perp to the media.

poppy loves. Elderly Jewish men who are potential robbery victims.

ANY ADDRESS WILL DO

It was a *really* busy day tour, and me and my partner, Talamo, are about to go to meal [cop talk for lunch] when we get a call about a road-rage incident. It came over as two motorists fighting in the street at a light. Since it was super busy that day, we barely had time for coffee in the morning, and we are now about six hours into our tour. So we figure we will handle it real quick, then grab something to eat.

We show up not knowing what to expect, and it turns out these two guys got into a very minor fender bender, but they got pissed at each other and started to wrestle in the middle of the street. We separate them and try to find out what happened. One guy cut the other off or had the right-of-way or some BS-type stuff, so it got heated, and they started yelling and pushing and shoving. Next thing you know, they are rolling around in the street holding up traffic. Nobody was hurt, so it's just a cross-complainant type of thing—paperwork but no arrest.

After we separated them, we took one guy's information and told him to wait where he was. We go to take the other guy's info, but he doesn't have a license on him. He tells us his name is Mitch Feinstein.

I say, "OK, Mitch. What's your address, date of birth, and Social Security number?"

He says, "I didn't do it."

"Didn't do what?"

"I wasn't fighting in the street. That wasn't me."

I look at my partner with an expression of "Did I just hear this guy right?"

So Talamo asks, "What are ya talkin' about? We just rolled up on you guys, and both of you were rollin' around in the middle of the street."

Mitch goes, "Yeah, it was my body, but it wasn't me. It was Lenny."

"What?" Talamo says. "Who the hell is Lenny?"

"That's my alter ego. I am a schizophrenic, and Lenny lives inside me."

"Wait a minute, let me get this straight," I said. "You're two people living in one body? You and Lenny—your alter ego?"

"Yeah, that's right."

We're starving at this point and just want to go to meal, so Talamo asks him, "OK, then what the hell is Lenny's address?"

So the guy pauses, leans over, and softly says, "OK, I'll give it to you, but don't tell Lenny you got it from me."

Then he looks back over both shoulders as if somebody is watching him and says, "If he found out I gave you his address, he'd be pissed. He can get a little crazy—he's not normal like you and me."

MORE 911 TALES

Dispatcher: "Nine-one-one, what is your emergency?"

Caller: "Someone broke into my house and took a bite out of my ham and cheese sandwich."

Dispatcher: "Excuse me?"

Caller: "I made a ham and cheese sandwich and left it on the kitchen table, and when I came back from the bathroom, someone had taken a bite out of it."

Dispatcher: "Was anything else taken?"

Caller: "No, but this has happened to me before, and I'm sick and tired of it!"

Dispatcher: "Nine-one-one, what is the nature of your emergency?"

Caller: "I'm trying to reach nine-eleven but my phone doesn't have an eleven on it."

Dispatcher: "This is nine-eleven."

Caller: "I thought you just said it was nine-one-one?"

Dispatcher: "Yes, ma'am, nine-one-one and nine-eleven are the same thing."

Caller: "Honey, I may be old, but I'm not stupid."

Dispatcher: "Nine-one-one, what's the nature of your emergency?"

Caller: "My wife is pregnant and her contractions are only two minutes apart."

Dispatcher: "Is this her first child?"

Caller: "No, you idiot! This is her husband!"

RAN OUT OF BULLETS

An illegal alien in Polk County, Florida, got pulled over in a routine traffic stop and ended up executing the deputy who stopped him. The deputy was shot eight times, including once behind his right ear at close range. Another deputy was wounded, and a police dog was killed. A statewide manhunt ensued.

The murderer was found hiding in a wooded area, and as soon as he took a shot at the SWAT team, officers opened fire on him. They hit the guy sixty-eight times. Naturally, the media went nuts and asked why they had to shoot the poor undocumented immigrant sixty-eight times.

Sheriff Grady Judd told the *Orlando Sentinel*, "Because that's all the ammunition we had."

ABOUT THE AUTHORS

Scott Baker is a former NYPD police officer and boxer. He and Tom Philbin also wrote *The Funniest Cop Stories Ever* and won a Quill and Badge Award in 2007 from the International Union of Police Associations for their unpublished manuscript, *A Warmer Shade of Blue*. Scott is now a boxing and fitness trainer, and he teaches and performs improv comedy all around the East Coast. He still lives in New York.

Tom Philbin is a longtime freelance writer of both fiction and nonfiction, including nine novels set in "Precinct Siberia," where misfit—and funny—cops are sent. Tom won his first Quill and Badge Award in 1997 for *Cop Speak: The Lingo of Law Enforcement and Crime*, and he is the only writer to win the award twice.